How to Make Money in Stocks

Entrepreneur Series

M. Usman, PhD.

Mendon Cottage Books

JD-Biz Publishing

Download Free Books!

http://MendonCottageBooks.com

Our books are available at

1. Amazon.com
2. Barnes and Noble
3. Itunes
4. Kobo
5. Smashwords
6. Google Play Books

Download Free Books!

http://MendonCottageBooks.com

Table of Contents

Introduction

You have a lot of options you can use to make money. But investing in the stock market is among the best that one can think of. By buying shares, you can double, triple, or even increase your investment by 10 times.

It all comes down to how you play you cards. If you invest in the right companies, you will just sit at home while your money works for you.

However, investing is not without risks.

In this book, you will learn how to make money buying stock. Although this is not easy, it is not as hard as you may think.

The book will start with an introduction to stocks and how you can make money with them. We will then move on to look at how much you need to get started; many mistakenly think they have to be filthy rich.

Profiting from your investment comes down to the strategies you use. If you follow the wrong ones, you will likely fail to achieve your goals. And in the worst cases, you may even lose your money. The book has a chapter dedicated to investing strategies.

With so many companies you can invest in, you may not know which ones are the best. But fear not as you will also find another chapter dedicated to analyzing companies.

In addition to all that, you will find other tips to increase your understanding on this subject. You will surely find the book helpful.

Enjoy the reading.

Chapter 1: Stocks 101

Buying stock of a certain company makes you a shareholder. And as such, you have a fraction of ownership in everything the business owns. If the company makes a profit, you receive a portion of those profits.

However, being a shareholder does not give you rights to demand whatever you want. Your rights are limited. For example, being a shareholder of Toyota doesn't mean you can test-drive new vehicles for free.

When you buy shares, you are given a certificate to represent them. However, this is held by your brokerage to ease trading of your shares.

You can only buy shares of publicly listed companies – the ones you see on the stock exchange. The opposite of these are private limited companies, which only issue shares to a select few (usually, the owners of the business).

Why Are Shares Issued

The moment you buy shares, you are a part owner of the business that issued them. Since it takes a lot of sweat and time to develop a successful business, you may wonder why issue stocks. If companies never did this, then its founders would keep all the profits for themselves.

The thing is that issuing shares is in the interest of every business. Although it comes with the sharing of profits, the benefits the business enjoys in return are massive.

Let's look at the following example:

ABC limited, a company involved in the manufacturing of Bluetooth keyboards, would like to expand and have a global presence. Since this is an ambitious project, it will need a lot of money, which the company does not have. So it has two choices: borrow the money or sell shares.

Borrowing will mean the money will have to be paid back. And on top of that, the company will also need to pay interest. Shares, on the other hand, won't have to be repaid. And there is no interest involved. If ABC Limited makes a profit, it will only need to share it with its shareholders.

From the above example, you can see that issuing shares is an attractive and effective way of raising capital. However, the process is not as simple as you may think. There are requirements that the company must fulfill before it can be listed on the stock exchange. In addition to that, the public must be convinced that it has a future; that's the only way they will put their money in it.

Types of Stock

Shares fall into a number of categories. Here are the most common:

Common Shares

These are the ones that most people invest in. Their biggest benefit is that they come with voting rights, enabling you to choose who must direct the company. Furthermore, you receive a dividend depending on the number of shares you own. However, the biggest drawback is that the dividends can fluctuate, which is a cause of concern for many.

Preferred Shares

These are not common. And unlike common shares, they do not usually have voting rights. Their biggest advantage is that you are guaranteed a fixed dividend forever. And most of the times, the dividend is higher than of common shares.

How You Can Make Money with Stocks

Basically, there are two ways on how you can make money with shares. Here they are:

1. Dividends

A dividend is the amount of money that a company takes from its profits to give to its shareholders. This amount is dependent on the amount of profit that the company makes. In addition, it is also dependent on the number of shares you hold.

For example, if the earning per share is $0.20 per share, 100 shares will bank you $20. And 1,000 shares will bring you $200. If you can add enough zeros to the number of shares you own, you can see how much potential this has.

However, dividends are not always guaranteed. The company can reduce them at any time. And in the worst cases, it can stop giving out dividends altogether. Usually, when a company does this, it is a sign of a trouble. And this is usually accompanied by falling stock prices as most investors abandon such companies.

2. Appreciation

This refers to when the price of your shares increases over time. For instance, if you bought stock a year ago at $1, and its share price increases to $2, you can make a profit of $1 for each share you sell. And this is how most investors make money on the market. They invest in shares of companies they expect to grow. And as the share price increases, they sell that stock.

This idea is supported by statistics which shows that the share price of most companies grows over time. When Microsoft went public in 1986, its share price was $21. This has increased over the years. Imagine how much return on investment this would have been if you had invested early.

How Much Do You Need To Get Started

This is not an easy question to answer. Partly, that's because each situation is different. In addition, everyone has different goals for investing. However, the good thing is that you don't need to be stinking rich to buy shares anymore. With the rise of the internet, most things have become cheaper. As a result, you can get started with as little as $500.

Chapter 2: Advantages and Disadvantages of Investing in Stock

Investing is without a doubt is good way to increase your income. However, that is not enough to persuade anyone to buy stock or any other form of investment.

In this chapter, we will look at the pros and cons of buying shares. While many think that it's all smiles in the stock market, the fact is that people do lose money in it.

Advantages:

1. Two ways of earning – like previously stated, you can earn by selling your stock or through dividends. And the best part is that these earnings are likely to increase if you invest in the right company. This double way of earning can result in greater returns on your investments than if you buy a house or other forms of securities.

2. Stocks are liquid – you can sell your shares for cash anytime at a fair price.

3. A good way of earning passive income – although you will need to assess the market as well as the companies to invest in, buying stock does not involve a lot of work. You do not need to be an active participant in making money like an employee or a member of management. If you invest right, you just need to hold your stock and enjoy the dividends as they come.

4. Limited liability – in case the company goes down, anything that belongs to it can be taken to repay its loans. However, although you own a stake in the company, your private property - house, cars, or anything valuable – will be safe. This is unlike partnerships or sole proprietors where personal property may also be taken.

Disadvantages

1. Stock prices always fluctuate – the price of your stock will always change depending on a number of factors. If it goes up, you have no reason to worry. But if the opposite happens, most investors panic as this can result in losses. Out of impulse, many sell their shares even if that was never the intention.

2. Risk of losing your money – if it was easy to tell what the future would be like, no investor would lose money in stocks. Unfortunately, nobody knows the future and this leads to investing in businesses likely to fail. So when you buy stock, always keep it in the back of your head that you may lose your money. Your best solution to this is to diversify your portfolio. This will mean losses in one company will be offset by gains in another.

3. You do not have full ownership – being a shareholder gives you some rights to the company. But these are limited. For example, you cannot call the manager of the company to tell him what he must do.

Chapter 3: Important Terms to Know

Every industry has a language that defines how those in it communicate. The same is the case with the stock market. Knowing the words you will need will accelerate your learning. But at the same time, it will ensure that you understand everything when trading. Needless to mention, this will also keep you from making silly mistakes as a result of ignorance.

Bear market – this is a term that refers to how investors feel about the market. Specifically, investors in a bear market have a perception that the price of stock will fall. The reasons for this can be many: struggling economy, dying industries, and poor management.

Bull market – this is the opposite of the bear market. And as such, it represents an outlook that the price of shares will increase. This belief is accompanied by heavy investment from people looking to increase their earnings.

Stock Exchange – a place where shares of different companies are traded.

RIO – in full, it means "Return on Investment." It is a representation of how much you earn as a percentage of your total investment. Usually, when you have a higher RIO, the investment is very risky.

	Stock
Bought: January 2010	$500
Sold: July 2010	$550
Profit	$50
RIO	10%

Portfolio – This is a term used to describe the collection of investments belonging to one person. It includes stocks, options, bonds, and mutual funds. Because the investment world is unpredictable and full of risk, it is important that you have a diversified portfolio. In other words, do not put all your eggs in one basket. One way to do this is to invest in at least two companies. Alternately, instead of only picking stock yourself, you can also invest in mutual funds.

P/E ratio – This is one important thing every investor needs to know. It looks at a company's share price in relation to its earnings per share. Despite this being an important metric, you must use it with other tools to get a better picture of whether a company is worth the investment. Use the following formulae to calculate the P/E ratio:

$$P/E = \frac{\text{Market Value Price per Share}}{\text{Earnings per Share}}$$

Security and equity – These are two terms that many use interchangeably. But that is wrong. Security means all types of investments. This can include bonds, stocks, and mutual funds. Equity specifically refers to shares.

Hedge – This is a practice investors use to protect their securities from risk. If you believe you will face a loss in a certain investment, you can make another one you believe will bring a profit to offset that loss.

Chapter 4: Getting Money in the Stock Market

You can put your money in the stock market in a number of ways. Your expertise, the amount of money you have, and your wiliness to learn are some of the things that determine how you do that.

Mutual Fund

This is the recommended way of investing for those with no experience in the stock market or those who don't plan to be active in it. A mutual fund is a collection of money from different investors that is spent on various investments. This enables the fund's members to enjoy benefits they wouldn't have if they had invested individually.

Every mutual fund has a manager. And he is the one responsible for when to buy or sell shares, which companies to invest in, and more. This removes the burden from the members of that fund – enabling them to focus on other aspects of their lives.

When you invest in a mutual fund, your money can work diversely. If the fund is invested in 10 companies, it means your money is also in all those companies.

Although there are a lot of advantages that come with mutual funds, the biggest is that your money is managed professionally. Fund managers, and anyone working with them, dedicates their time mastering how to best invest money. You, on the other hand, have another job you worry about. So investing is something you will likely treat as a part-time job.

The only thing that may concern is that you lose control of decision making. And if you think that is a big problem, then you will need to…

Pick Stock Yourself

If you are ready to master what investing in stock is all about, then it helps to be at the helm of all investing decisions. However, doing this translates into hours of learning, observing, and practicing.

Choosing a Broker

By picking stock yourself, you have a requirement to hire a broker. And when it comes to this, you have two choices: traditional or online broker.

Traditional Broker

These are dedicated professionals who know the ropes of investing in stocks. Unlike a fund manager who decides what to do with your money, these people are only there to offer advice. This may include the companies to invest in, when to sell or buy stock, and notifications on upcoming opportunities.

Because of this customized service, these people charge high commissions.

If you are not confident about learning all there is about stocks, this is probably the best way to go.

Online Brokers

Almost everything can now be done online. So it is not surprising that you can also have an online broker. Unlike the traditional ones, these are cheaper. Mainly, that's because the services you receive are generic despite that everyone has different needs.

An online broker gives you all the information it deems necessary for your investment decisions. And it's up to you to make sense of that information and determine how to use it.

Because of this, going this route means you must be ready to learn all you can about stock trading. In addition, you must actively observe the market.

Things to Keep in Mind When Looking for a Broker

Your brokerage firm is not only there to give you advice on the best investment choices as it also carries out your orders. But most importantly, it handles your money; therefore, it is important that you do not make mistakes here. Choosing the right broker is the first step to being successful in the stock market. Here are some things you must keep in mind:

Experience – this applies to traditional brokers. If you are going to base your decisions on someone's advice, that someone must have a good idea of what he is saying. Otherwise, he may mislead you with his inept advice.

Reputation – experience aside, your broker must have a good record of helping people. Reports of scams, poor quality services, or anything that may jeopardize your success must be thoroughly looked at before you reach a decision.

Fees – this is a very important area you must never overlook. For starters, remember that cheap usually comes with a low-quality service. But that should not force you to go for the most expensive broker. Before you make a decision, compare fees of different brokers.

But before you even do that, sit down and think of what you want from a broker. This will help you to not go for butterflies (services you don't need) and waste money in the process. In addition, it will also help you to decide between a traditional and online broker.

Lastly, you must dive under the water to discover the hidden fees. Most brokers only show the cheaper services while hiding the expensive ones. They then slap you with them in the face after you have comfortably sat in their boat.

Availability – if going for an online broker, you must ensure that its website is always online all the time. You do not want to miss something important just because you can't access your account.

Customer support – again, this is another thing that applies to online brokers. Since everything you get is generic, you will have questions about some things. And your broker must always be there to provide answers. More than that, he must provide them in a timely manner.

To find this out, you can fake a question to see your broker's response time.

Chapter 5: Investing Strategies

As you saw in chapter 1, you can make money from stocks by selling it or through dividends.

If eying dividends, the basis of your strategy will be "buy and hold." With this, you buy stock and keep it until the time you will need your money. Usually, anyone following this has a long-term goal he would like to fulfill; for example, saving for retirement, wanting to buy a house, etc. Analysts agree that holding stock for long periods of time is a good way to increase the return on your investment.

The best part with this is that as long as you choose a good company, you can focus on other things than your stock. If the share price drops, you won't panic as these are usually short-term nuisances. Not only will this keep you from unnecessary stress, but you will not be forced to sell your shares out of fear.

In addition, by maintaining a long term position on you stock, you minimize commissions that can eat your profit.

The company you invest in must be one you believe will be around for a foreseeable future. At the same time, it must show potential for growth, which will translate into growth of your dividends as well as an increase in share price.

In another scenario, your focus may not be on dividends, but selling your stock when it appreciates. As a result, you will invest money in shares that are selling for low, hoping to profit when their prices rise.

This strategy is great if you actively monitor the stock market. In fact, you can make a lot of money in a relatively short time if you play your cards right.

However, one of the drawbacks is that you must be dedicated and knowledgeable. You must be able to accurately determine the movement of the market at any time.

Another disadvantage with strategies based on this is that the risk of losing your money is high: you will be buying and selling shares of different companies every year. Some of these will be successful while others will fail.

Adding to that, trading actively will accumulate a lot of fees in commissions that you won't have if you just hold the stock.

Here are some of the investing strategies you can follow on the stock market:

Growth

An investor who follows this strategy looks for companies with the highest growth of earnings per share. The argument is that investors want high dividends. And as such, will fight for companies that are seen to be growing their earnings per share. This consequently raises that company's share price.

So if you can buy early, you will pay low and be able to sell high later.

Unfortunately, most companies that fall in this category are highly valued; therefore, you will still pay more to acquire the shares than if you follow another strategy.

Another consideration is that most of these companies are young. And there is no guarantee that they will grow to become household names. Here is something to keep in mind all the time: for every Microsoft, there are a thousands other Microsofts that fail.

Value

Investors in this category are also known as bargain hunters; they are on the lookout for stock that is selling at what they consider attractive or low prices. Normally, these investors have a bullish behavior, convinced that the price of the shares will rise in future. And if they are right, the gains from this strategy can be massive.

The only risky part is that value shares are usually out of favor with most investors. The reasons for this could be because of a dying industry, reports of declining earnings per share, or some other horrible reasons.

Income

Some investors just want a guarantee that they will get dividends when the time is due. And this is only possible by investing in big, established businesses, with high prices per share. These high prices usually also come with high dividends.

Unfortunately, this strategy means you need to have a lot of money.

Dollar Cost Averaging

For new investors, the biggest worry is investing a lot of money at the wrong time. And this happens a lot as most newbies lack the expertise to identify where the market may go next.

A solution to this is to use the dollar cost averaging strategy.

You first determine an amount you will invest in a company of your choice over time. For example, you can choose to invest $500 in ZXC Limited every six months for 4 years. So every January and July, you will be buying shares from ZXC worth $500. This will disregard the share price at the moment, or what you think if may be if you wait for a month.

When the share price is low, you will buy more shares. And when it is high, you will buy fewer shares. You will you take advantage of the lowest prices and average out when you buy at higher prices.

Here is an example to illustrate this:

Imagine you want to invest in RTT Limited. Using the cost dollar averaging strategy, you have resolved to invest $100 per month for 5 months. Here is a table showing how this will play out.

Month	Price per share ($)	Shares Purchased	Accumulative number of shares	Average cost per share ($)
January	25	8	8	25
February	20	10	18	22.22
March	33	6	24	24.92
April	40	5	29	27.57
May	25	8	37	26.97

As you can see, even when the share price rises to $40, your average price per share stays below $30.

On IPOs

IPO stands for Initial Public Offering. And it's when a company that was privately owned goes public. Usually, shares of such companies are still cheaper with potential for growth. For example, going back to the example of Microsoft, if you had invested in an IPO, you would have spent only $21 per share. And now, you would be rich.

That is what gets a lot of people's blood boiling.

However, IPOs usually make bad investments; therefore, it is in your best interest that you avoid them.

The thing is that getting on an IPO is not easy. When a company wants to go public, it sells lots of shares to an investment firm. The investment firm gets the shares to brokers who know clients.

Unfortunately for you, brokers don't have time to convince individuals to invest in a company that is going public – that would be inefficient and ineffective. So they go to big institutions capable of buying lots of shares at a time. As such, there is nothing left for ordinary people like you and me. In fact, even managers of some big mutual funds do not get any IPOs.

If you have an opportunity to get on an IPO, chances are that no one wants those shares. And you should question your logic if you are the only one who does. IPOs of better companies are not easy to get on. And this is what makes IPOs bad investments for ordinary people as we have to settle for ordinary companies.

Remember, for every successful company that goes public, there are a lot of other companies that crumble to the ground. You do not want to crumble with them.

Chapter 6: Fundamental and Technical Analysis

Charts, calculators, and the news are going to become your next best friend as you get ready to buy stock. All this will be in an effort to determine which companies on the exchange are best to invest in. Without this crucial analysis, you will end up putting your money in the wrong company.

Fundamental and technical analysis are the two tools you can use in this process. They lie on opposing ends of the line and you must choose which side you will face. However, most experts recommend that you must combine these two for better results.

Fundamental Analysis

This is the study of a company focusing on factors affecting it and how these could hinder growth. Investors agree that your money is best invested in companies that are increasing profits and share prices. At the same time, these companies must keep borrowing low and show signs of keeping a consistent growth pattern.

Things to focus on:

Performance – how a company has been performing can tell a great deal of how it will be like in future. As already said, you must focus on growth in profits, share prices, and revenue. And this is easy to find out as you can look at profit statements, balance sheets, etc.

Management – these are the people in the driver's seat. If they are not qualified, they will drive everyone on board into a ditch.

Industry – this also determines if a company has a future. For example, investing in a business focused on making tape recorders won't take you anywhere in this day and age.

The economy – it is one of the most important things as it affects all companies regardless of what industry they are in. So it's necessary that you stay alert on where the economy is heading at all times.

A decline in the economy affects businesses negatively. For example, rising unemployment will reduce consumer spending because people will have no money to buy things. Every penny in their pockets will go towards the essentials. So companies serving non-essential goods, like leisure, will be hit the worst.

The opposite happens if the economy is thriving. As such, share prices increase, letting investors profit from their risky endeavors.

Usually, fundamental analysis is done in a top-down approach – you start with the big picture and narrow it to the little details. You can do this by first looking at the entire market to determine products that are doing well. You would then move on to a specific sector after which you would zoom in on a specific industry. Upon further analysis, you can focus on a certain region and then pick a few companies to analyze.

The point here it to recognize the market direction and determine companies that may be worth more in future. However, although you may put a lot of hours into this, it does not mean that your predictions will turn out right.

Technical Analysis

Unlike fundamental analysis, this is mainly about reading charts. You do this to identify trends, whether upward or downward, in the price of shares. It's the reason technical analysis is also called chart reading.

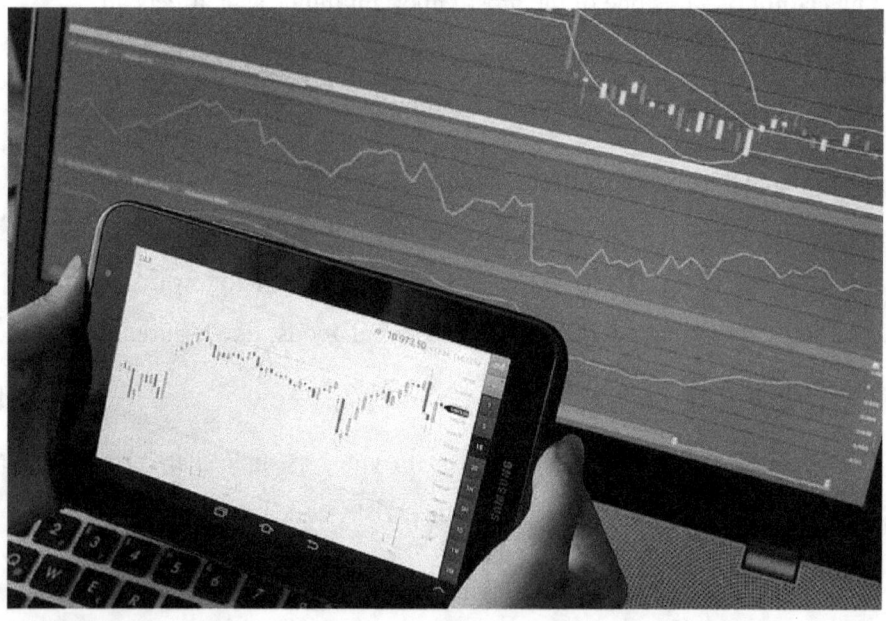

The belief is that the price of stock does not just change anyhow – there are specific factors that influence it. These could be the economy, industry, or management of the company. Since these influences are already factored into the charts, you have no need to look at them again.

For example, you may realize that during certain times of the year, the stock price of a certain company drops and then picks up again. If you invest in this company while the price is low, you can profit when the price rises again.

On paper, technical analysis may seem simple – but it is far from that. When you look at the charts, you need to create further ratios for better decisions.

However, these methods aside, you will need to keep your eyes open at all times. Companies or industries with growth potential will not always tower above your head like the sun. Sometimes, they are the garage businesses nobody has ever heard of. If you can analyze these and see that they are worth the investment, you may land yourself a nice deal.

Conclusion

First, thank you for reading the book. Having come this far, the recommendation is that you must keep learning about investing in the stock market.

If you will be picking stock yourself, it means you will be competing against others who have been in the industry for years, with a universe of tricks to play the game in their favor. It's only by knowing all you can about stocks that you can stand up to these guys.

If there is something you would like to know, search for it on the internet. In addition, it does not hurt to ask the pros for advice.

However, the one thing you must never do is to base your investment decision on the recommendations of analysts. Most of the times, these recommendations are never true.

You must not forget to factor in taxation in your earnings when you start trading. If you are not careful, this can slowly eat your earnings. Since this is a long and complicated subject, it's advisable that you hire a tax advisor.

And lastly, thanks to the advances in technology, you can practice your investing skills without putting any money in people's hands. There are a lot of online simulators that imitate buying stock. Making them better, they use real market conditions, just that the money is fake. By using these, you can have a good idea of whether you are ready to start trading or not.

About the Author

Dr. Usman is an MD, now pursuing his post-graduation degree. As a medical doctor, he has deep insight in all aspects of health, fitness and nutrition.

He is a certified nutritionist and a personal trainer. With these qualifications, he has helped countless people reach their health, fitness and weight loss goals.

Dr. Usman is an avid researcher with 20+ publications in internationally accepted peer reviewed journals.

He is an accomplished writer with more than 5 years of writing experience. In this time, he has produced countless blogs, articles and research work on topics related to health, fitness and nutrition.

He is a published author with more than 100+ books published and several more in the pipe line.

Finally, he runs his own blog and posts health, fitness and nutrition related articles there regularly. You can visit his blog at http://hcures.com/

You can reach out to him via email at usman92yasin@gmail.com

Check out some of the other JD-Biz Publishing books

Gardening Series on Amazon

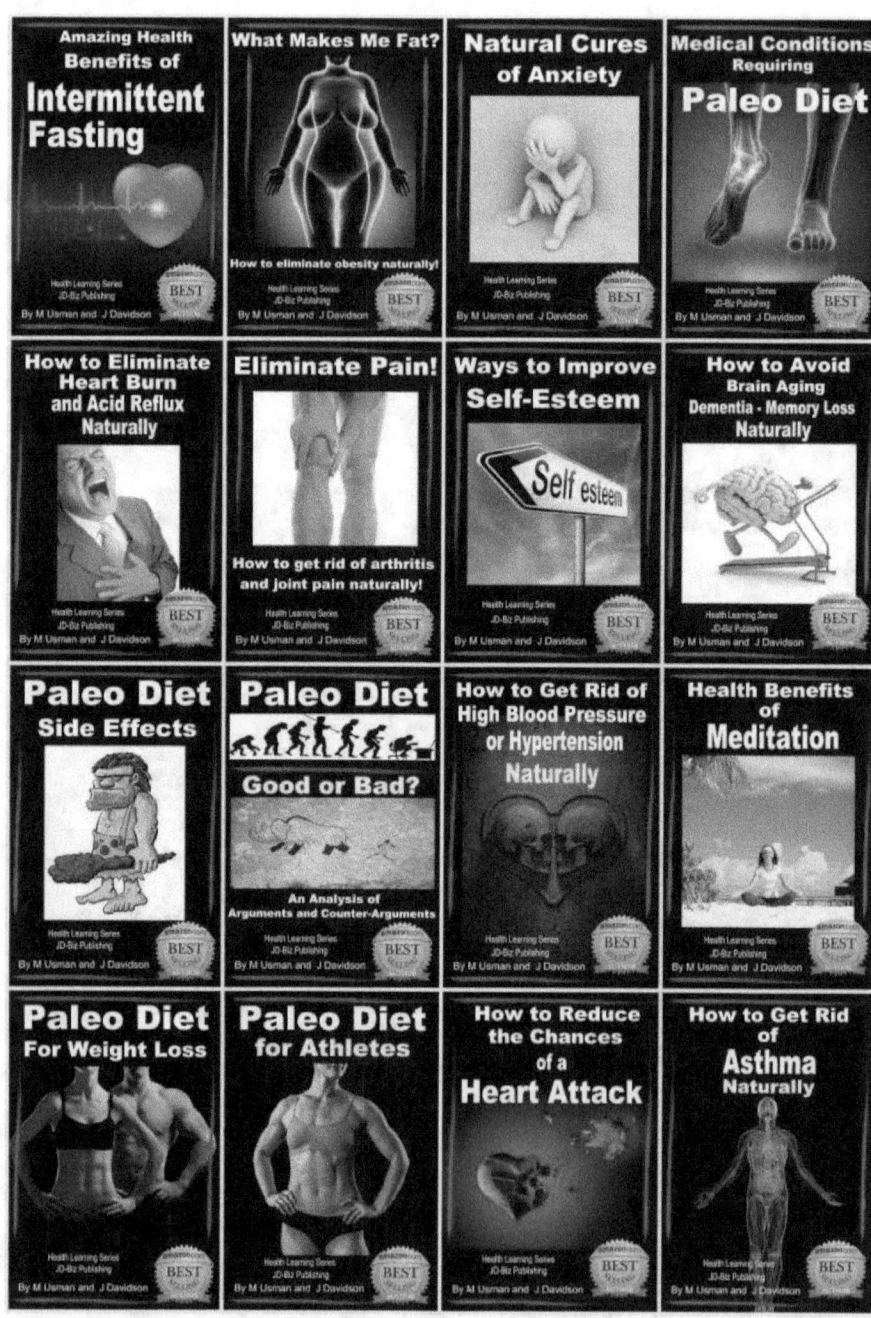

Amazing Animal Book Series

Learn To Draw Series

How to Build and Plan Books

Entrepreneur Book Series

Our books are available at

1. Amazon.com

2. Barnes and Noble

3. Itunes

4. Kobo

5. Smashwords

6. Google Play Books

Download Free Books!

http://MendonCottageBooks.com

Publisher

JD-Biz Corp

P O Box 374

Mendon, Utah 84325

http://www.jd-biz.com/

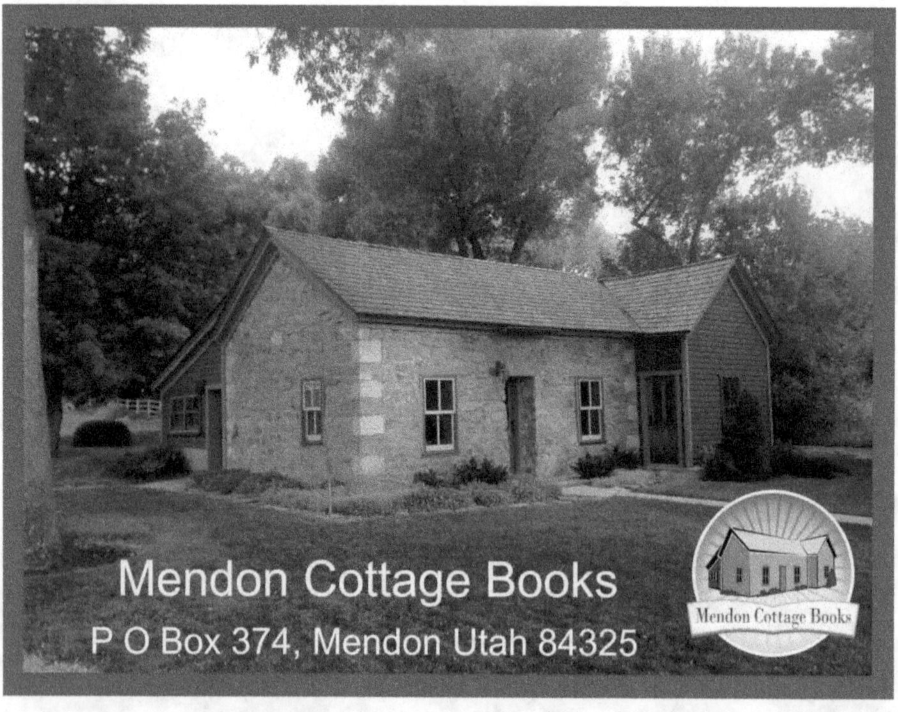

Mendon Cottage Books

P O Box 374, Mendon Utah 84325

www.ingramcontent.com/pod-product-compliance
Lightning Source LLC
Chambersburg PA
CBHW071831200526
45169CB00018B/1327